Time Passes

TIME PASSES

 Blair | HAIKU

 Kimmy Tran | ZEN INK

Airen Press
MADISON, WISCONSIN

WITH THANKS TO

KIMMY TRAN | Calligrapher, Chicago
whose Zen Ink renderings give the haiku voice

KAREN BICKERS | Alpha Graphics, Madison
for her steady advice and support

CURT CARPENTER | Designer, Aspen
for his creative energy

KAREN JOHNSON MATHEWS | for being

BLAIR MATHEWS © 2022
All Rights Reserved

ISBN: 978-1-7376436-1-6

 Airen Press

1240 Wellesley Road | Madison, WI 53705
bmathews@wisc.edu

CONTENTS

Wake	1
Once Upon a Time	3
Chapel	5
Constant	7
Equanimity	9
Galaxy	11
Hands	13
Heavy	15
Invitation	17
Passing	19
Patience	21
Perspective	23
Glimpse	25
Same	27

Still	29
Suddenly	31
Weathered	33
Vortex	35
Sign	37
Next	39
Wind	41
Blink	43
Incubation	45
Travelers	47
Place	49
Gift	51
Aging	53
Change	55

Wake

Seeds of fate,

Intention, attention,

Patience, forbearance,

Will, timing,

Awake.

Once Upon a Time

Born in time's

Black womb,

Breached into

Bare self's

Burnt light.

Chapel

Filtered light

Fills quiet space,

Full of yesterday's

Hopes, dreams,

Today's reality.

Constant

Prayer wheel spinning,

Yesterday,

Today,

Tomorrow,

Prayer wheel spinning,

Clarifying yesterday,

Calming now,

Tomorrow nonexistent.

Sights, sounds, smells,

Wind blowing

Afternoon rain,

Wind blowing

Mind clear,

Prayer wheel spinning.

Equanimity

Flitting dragonfly,

Whistling hawk,

Morning light,

Night sky,

Newborn's cry,

Dying sigh,

Laughter, tears,

Youth, years,

Know, wonder,

Just being,

Here, now,

Alive.

Galaxy

Night sky constellations

Swirl past Chimney Rock,

Jupiter pauses over

Thunder Mountain's

Lizard Rock,

Coyote time.

Hands

Father, Son,

Holding early

Morning hands,

Heading toward

School bus,

Life.

Heavy

Fog glued

To ground,

Waiting for Spring

To lift spirits.

Invitation

Predawn rain

Raps on window,

Spring sound,

Wondering sound,

Drips down sill.

Passing

Light snow

Melts in morning sun,

Puffy white clouds

Rest in mountain's

Crevices, corners,

Delicate Chinese

Brush painting.

Patience

Wind wipes

Recollections,

Weathered memories,

Through time worn

Rock crevices,

Clarity comes

In due time.

Perspective

Unadorned perch,

Worn reminder,

Time's parade

Passes in

Restful light.

Glimpse

Eyes burn,

Too many

Untold stories

Seen.

Same

Respectful bow,

Hesitant handshake,

Wanting contact.

Fellow travelers

Spanning cultures,

Seeking contact.

Time travelers

Reaching out

Along way ~

Still

Pebble drops

Into placid pond,

Ripples stir

Children's laughter,

Heartfelt tears,

Still there after

All these years.

Suddenly

Sunbeam

Pierces dew drop,

Casts

Rainbow

Shadow.

Weathered

Worn, wet

Work gloves

Hang limply,

Drying,

Waiting.

Toil tired

Worn body

Rests in

Next moment's

Shadow.

Vortex

Old friend passes,

Great Granddaughter borne,

Same time,

Same place,

Life's vortex.

Sign

Great Horned Owls,

Perched in pine,

Soft yodel sound,

Night time lovers,

Then quiet time.

Passage

Spirit rests on

Time's raft,

Carried into Cedar Falls,

Ready for quiet pool,

After rapid's din.

Next

Moving on

While still

Resting in now,

Walking in

Other's shadow.

Wind

Slowly blow

Dusty person,

Resting under

Yesterday's layers,

Good bye,

Hello.

Blink

Yesterday, hello,

Today, goodbye,

Each contact full,

Each moment whole,

No regrets.

Incubation

Deep thoughts

Sink in,

Lost in

Time's place,

Resting, waiting.

Travelers

Past boundaries — space, time,

Hooded mysteries of the mind,

Fly toward inner reaches,

Quiet retrospective place,

Where journey ends,

Begins.

Place

Learning to love,

Beyond thinking,

Becoming present,

Being real,

Being love.

Gift

Death's shadow,

Invitation to

Release hard grip,

Softly embrace

Life, beloved.

Aging

Removing

Conditioning's

Cloak,

Child like.

Change

Now Spring,

Then Summer,

Now young,

Then old,

Change changes.

Brown marsh grass

Sways in chilled breeze,

October sun warms

Face cooled by

Chilled breeze.

Today's times,

Warm, cold, changed,

External bearings

Torn, blown away,

Rooting deep within.

Time to be simple,

Look self, others

In the eye,

Love fully,

Pass quietly.

www.ingramcontent.com/pod-product-compliance
Lightning Source LLC
Chambersburg PA
CBHW040108120526
44589CB00040B/2825